Language Arts
Grade 1

TABLE OF CONTENTS

Page Number(s)

CONSONANTS & VOWEL SOUNDS

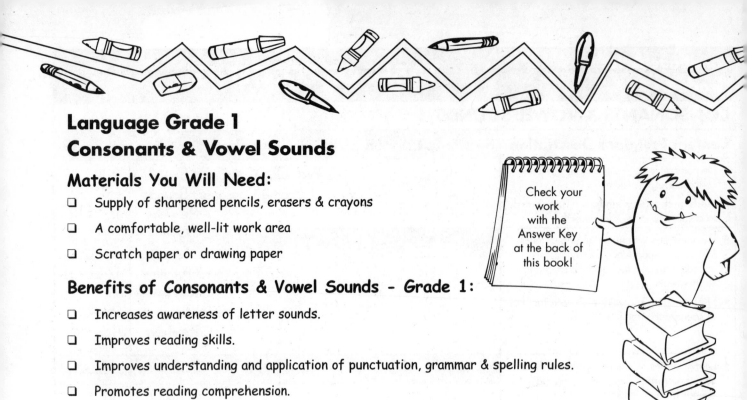

Language Grade 1
Consonants & Vowel Sounds

Materials You Will Need:
- ❑ Supply of sharpened pencils, erasers & crayons
- ❑ A comfortable, well-lit work area
- ❑ Scratch paper or drawing paper

Check your work with the Answer Key at the back of this book!

Benefits of Consonants & Vowel Sounds - Grade 1:
- ❑ Increases awareness of letter sounds.
- ❑ Improves reading skills.
- ❑ Improves understanding and application of punctuation, grammar & spelling rules.
- ❑ Promotes reading comprehension.
- ❑ Encourages shared reading experiences.
- ❑ Allows you to have fun with language!

Parent & Teacher Coaching Tips:
- ❑ *Prepare.* Provide your child with a quiet, well-lit place to study. Include a desk or table with an upright chair that is comfortable. Make sure that your child has plenty of room to work and spread out materials.
- ❑ *Schedule.* Choose a time that seems to work well for your child. Select a time when you and your child are able to focus on learning together. Be sure to allow a break from working after a long school day.
- ❑ *Engage.* Use your child's learning strengths and interests to build skills. Allow your child to act out, draw, verbalize, play, move and listen to help build skills. Encourage your child to think of games, activities and ideas that can help to reinforce concepts.
- ❑ *Break.* Children need frequent study breaks. Look for the Stop sign throughout the book, then encourage your child to get up, stretch, move, run, have a snack, or try a new activity for a while. Return to the workbook when your child is ready.
- ❑ *Relax!* You are a critical influence in helping your child to feel relaxed and ready to learn. Help your child to: eat well, get plenty of rest, relax, visualize success, and release energy in a physical way (i.e. running, walking, playing sports). Practice deep-breathing, drawing, meditation, and encourage your child to practice other ways to relax.
- ❑ *Talk.* Encourage your child to talk about any feelings related to test-anxiety, help your child understand the need for tests and stress the value of <u>real</u> learning that is not always obvious with test scores. Encourage your child to express feelings through drawings, role play activities, puppets, or however he or she chooses!

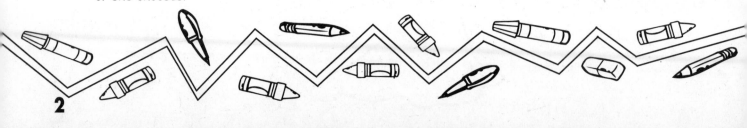

Say the name of each picture.
Color the tigers and the sun.

 Draw a line from the tigers to each picture that has the same beginning sound as **tigers**. Draw a line from the sun to each picture that has the same beginning sound as **sun**.

 Challenge: Make a consonant picture book. Find pictures of things that begin with the sound of **s** or **t**. Look in magazines, advertisements, newspapers, greeting cards, and so on.

Ss

 Tt

*Recognizing the initial consonant sounds of **Tt** and **Ss***

Say the name of each picture.
Color the bear and the heart.

 Draw a line from the bear to each picture that has the same beginning sound as **bear**. Draw a line from the heart to each picture that has the same beginning sound as **heart**.

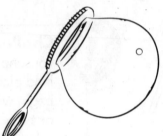

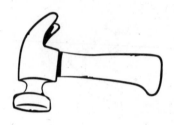

Bb

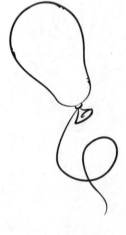

Hh

Say the name of each picture.
Color the monkeys and the kangaroo.

 Draw a line from the monkeys to each picture that has the same beginning sound as **monkeys**. Draw a line from the kangaroo to each picture that has the same beginning sound as **kangaroo**.

Mm

Kk

 Challenge: Add to your consonant picture book with things that begin with the sound of **m** or **k**. Draw some of your own pictures, too!

Say the name of each picture.
Color the juggler and the fox.

 Draw a line from the juggler to each picture that has the same beginning sound as **juggler**. Draw a line from the fox to each picture that has the same beginning sound as **fox**.

Ff

Jj

Recognizing the initial consonant sounds of **Jj** and **Ff**

Say the name of each picture.
Color the giraffe and the goose.
Draw a line from the giraffe to each picture that has the same beginning sound as **giraffe**. Draw a line from the goose to each picture that has the same beginning sound as **goose**.

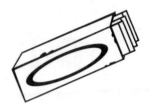

Gg

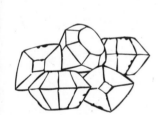

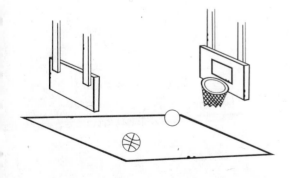

Say the name of each picture. Color the **dinosaur** green and the **lion** yellow. Color the rest of the pictures using the code.

Same beginning sound as **dinosaur** = (green)

Same beginning sound as **lion** = (yellow)

Dd     **Ll**

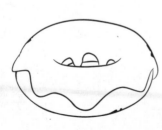   

Tip:
You can find more new words that begin like **dinosaur** and **lion** in a dictionary!

Say the name of each picture.
 Color the nails and the wood.
 Draw a line from the nails to each picture that has the same beginning sound as **nails**. Draw a line from the wood to each picture that has the same beginning sound as **wood**.

Ww

 Nn

Hard Sound

When **c** comes before **a**, **o**, or **u**, it has a hard sound like **k**.

<u>c</u>at   <u>cu</u>b   <u>co</u>t

Soft Sound

When **c** comes before **e**, **i**, or **y**, it has a soft sound like **s**.

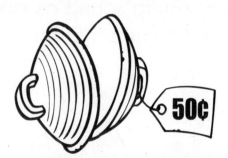

pri<u>ce</u>   <u>ce</u>nts
<u>cy</u>mbal

   Say each word. Circle the word if it has the soft **c** sound like **cents**. Draw a box around the word if it has the hard **c** sound like **cat**.

celery

car

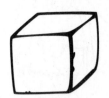

cup

cone

mice

cube

fence

comb

lace

Name:_____ Date:_____

  Say the name of each picture. Color the **rocket** red and the **panda** pink. Color the rest of the pictures using the code.

Same beginning sound as **rocket** = red

Same beginning sound as **panda** = pink

Challenge: Play *I Spy*! Look around you. Find something that begins with the same sound as **rocket** or **panda**. Ask someone to guess what it is!

Pp   **Rr**

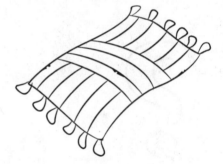

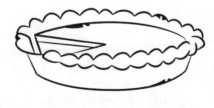

Say the name of each picture.
Color the queen and the violin.

 Draw a line from the queen to each picture that has the same beginning sound as **queen**. Draw a line from the violin to each picture that has the same beginning sound as **violin**.

Tip:
When words begin with the letter **q**, the letter **u** comes right after it, like queen, quarter, quiet, and question!

Qq

Vv

Name:_____ Date:_____

 Say the name of each picture. Listen for the sound of **x** at the end of each word. When **x** is at the end of a word it makes the sounds of **ks**.

si<u>x</u>

fo<u>x</u>

When it is at the beginning of a word, **x** often makes the same sound as **z**.

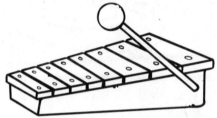

<u>x</u>ylophone

   Say the name of each picture. Draw a line from the picture to the correct word. Then, color the pictures.

box

ox

ax

tux

Recognizing the two consonant sounds of **Xx**

Say the name of each picture. Color the **yak** orange and the **zoo** blue. Color the rest of the pictures using the code.

Same beginning sound as **yak** =  orange

Same beginning sound as **zoo** = blue

 **Yy**

Zz

Say the name of each picture. Listen to the ending sound. Color in the circle next to the word that has the same ending sound as the picture.

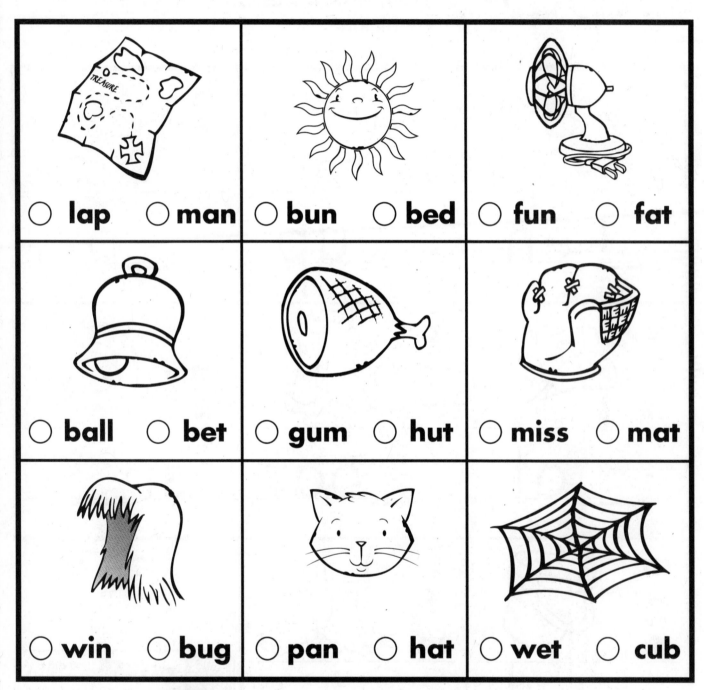

○ **lap**   ○ **man**   ○ **bun**   ○ **bed**   ○ **fun**   ○ **fat**

○ **ball**   ○ **bet**   ○ **gum**   ○ **hut**   ○ **miss**   ○ **mat**

○ **win**   ○ **bug**   ○ **pan**   ○ **hat**   ○ **wet**   ○ **cub**

 Challenge: Choose a word from this page. Think of 3 more words that end with the same sound as the word you picked! Try to write the words!

Recognizing the sounds of consonants in the final position

Name:_____   Date:_____

Review: Beginning & Ending Consonant Sounds

Circle the letter that is missing letter from each word. Then, write the letter to finish the word. Color the pictures.

h **m** **t**	**c** **p** **s**	**b** **f** **s**
___en	___up	___ox
b **c** **h**	**b** **c** **m**	**f** **m** **x**
___at	___oat	si___
m **p** **s**	**b** **f** **m**	
___ail	___eet	STOP! TAKE A BREAK! You did a great job! Place your Book Mark here & RELAX!

16   Review: Beginning & Ending Consonant Sounds

 **apple**    **b_a_t**

Apple and **bat** have the short **a** sound.

  Say the name of each picture. If you hear the short **a** sound, write **a** to finish the word. Say the words.

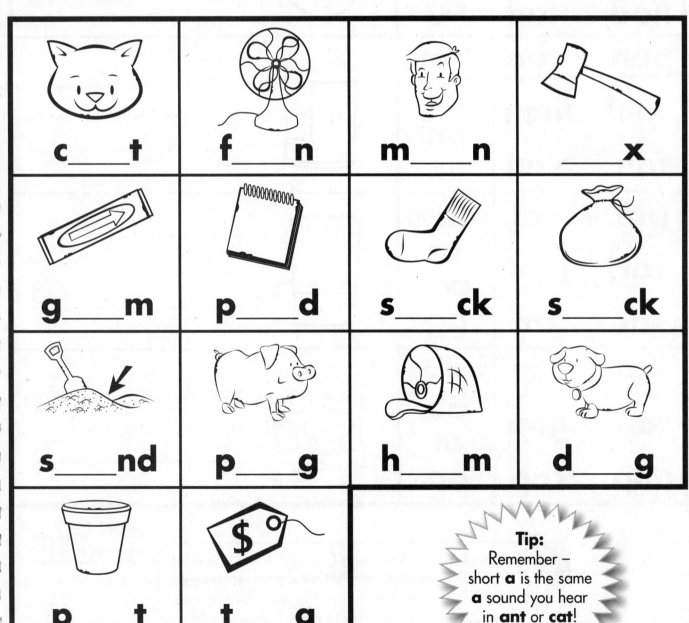

c__t   f__n   m____n   ____x

g____m   p____d   s____ck   s____ck

s____nd   p____g   h____m   d____g

p____t   t____g

Tip:
Remember –
short **a** is the same
a sound you hear
in **ant** or **cat**!

Say the rhyming words in the first box. Circle the letters that make the ending sound. Use the picture clue to write one more rhyming word.

bad	mad	**ending** ab ad ag	_____ - - - - - - - - - - _____
dad	pad		
had	lad		

pan	ran	**ending** ad an ax	_____ - - - - - - - - - - _____
tan	man		
fan	van		

pat	rat	**ending** at am ag	_____ - - - - - - - - - - _____
fat	mat		
sat	cat		

lap	rap	**ending** ab at ap	_____ - - - - - - - - - - _____
tap	gap		
nap	cap		

Challenge: Play *Presto Chango!* Think of a word that ends with **ag**, **am**, **at**, or **ap**. Then change the first letter and make another word that rhymes with your new word. Try to make 4 new words!

 **igloo**

 **dig**

The words **igloo** and **dig** have the short **i** sound.

  Say the name of each picture. If you hear the short **i** sound, write **i** to finish the word. Say the words you made.

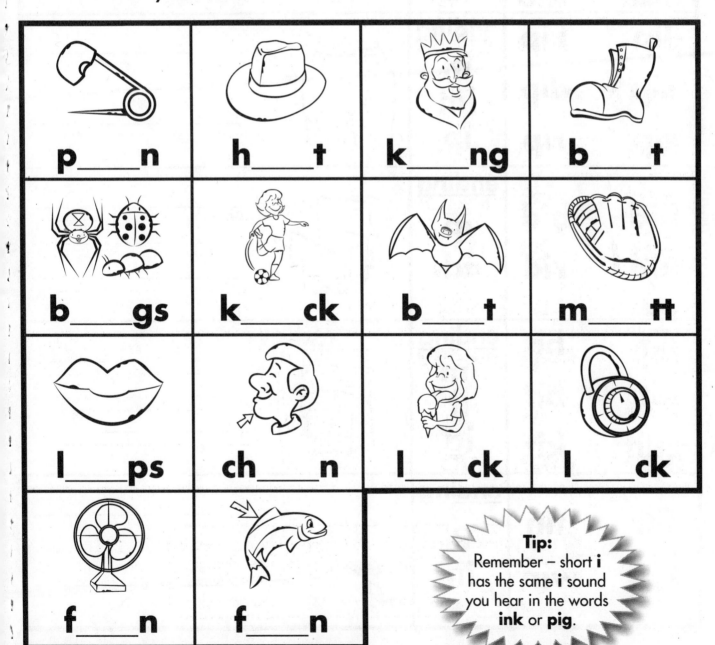

p___n	h___t	k___ng	b___t
b___gs	k___ck	b___t	m___tt
l___ps	ch___n	l___ck	l___ck
f___n	f___n		

Tip:
Remember – short **i** has the same **i** sound you hear in the words **ink** or **pig**.

Recognizing the sound of short **i**

Say the rhyming words in the first box. Circle the letters that make the ending sound. Use the picture clue to write one more rhyming word.

big	dig	**ending** it in ig		_____ _____ _____
fig	jig			
rig	wig			
lip	zip	**ending** in im ip		_____ _____ _____
sip	dip			
tip	rip			
hid	bid	**ending** ip id		_____ _____ _____
kid	rid			
lit	hit	**ending** im it ig		_____ _____ _____
fit	bit			
quit	kit			
fin	tin	**ending** it in		_____ _____ _____
kin	win			

Name:_____   Date:_____

up ⬆   **bug**

The words **up** and **bug** have the short **u** sound.

  Say the name of each picture. If you hear the short **u** sound, write **u** to finish the word. Say the words you made.

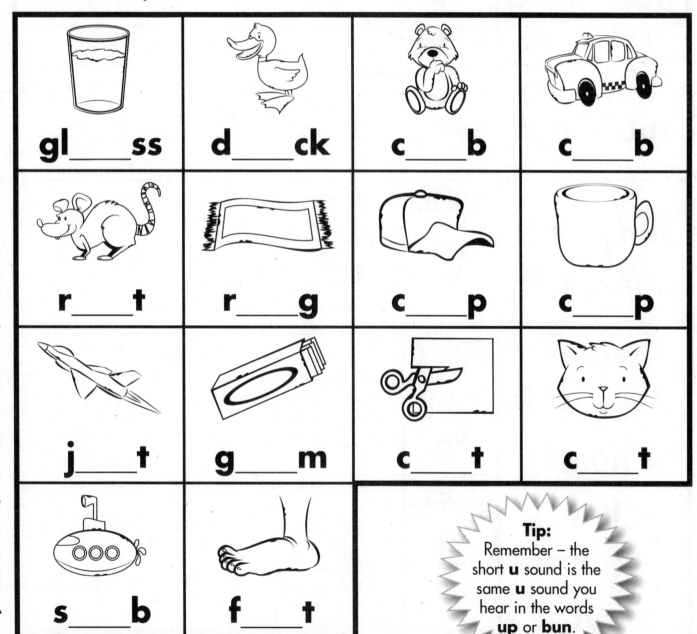

gl___ss   d___ck   c___b   c___b

r___t   r___g   c___p   c___p

j___t   g___m   c___t   c___t

s___b   f___t

Tip:
Remember – the short **u** sound is the same **u** sound you hear in the words **up** or **bun**.

Say the rhyming words in the first box. Circle the letters that make the ending sound. Use the picture clue to write one more rhyming word.

rug tug hug dug bug mug	ending ub ug up	_____
cub sub rub hub	ending ub ud	_____
fun run bun pun	ending un ug	_____
sum bum hum	ending um un	_____
hut but cut	ending ut ud	_____

 **ox**    **sock**

The words **ox** and **sock** have the short **o** sound.

  Say the name of each picture. If you hear the short **o** sound, write **o** to finish the word. Say the words you made.

p___g	b___x	m___p	h___ll
cl___ck	s___d	s___b	d___ck
p___p	b___g	c___t	c___t
f___x	d___sk		

Tip:
Remember – the short **o** sound is the same **o** as the sound you hear in **ox** and **block**.

Say the rhyming words in the first box. Circle the letters that make the ending sound. Use the picture clue to write one more rhyming word.

		ending	
bob	**mob**	**ob**	
sob	**rob**	**op**	
hop	**mop**	**od**	
pop	**sop**	**op**	
lot	**got**	**on**	
rot	**not**	**og**	
pot	**hot**	**ot**	
dock	**sock**	**ock**	
flock	**rock**	**ogs**	
dog	**bog**	**og**	
fog	**hog**	**op**	

egg **bell**

The words **egg** and **bell** have the short **e** sound.

 Say the name of each picture. If you hear the short **e** sound, write **e** to finish the word. Say the words you made.

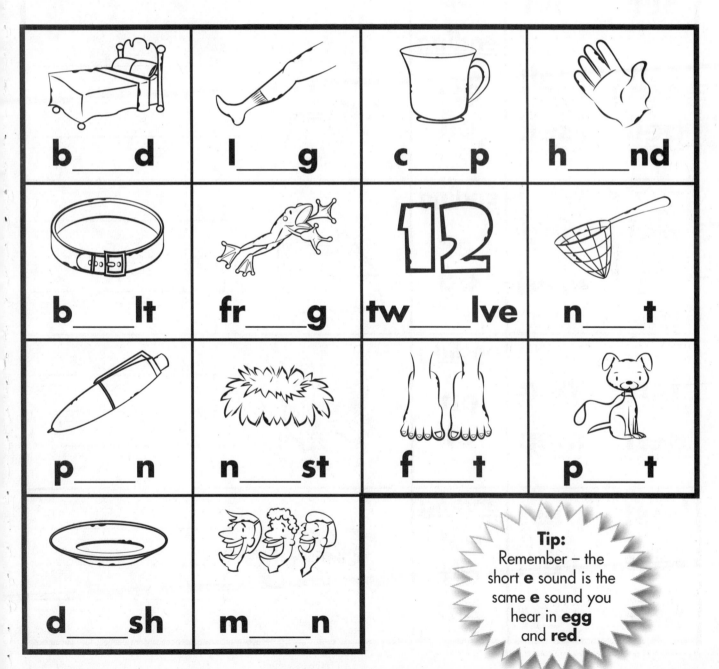

b___d   l___g   c___p   h___nd

b___lt   fr___g   tw___lve   n___t

p___n   n___st   f___t   p___t

d___sh   m___n

Tip:
Remember – the short **e** sound is the same **e** sound you hear in **egg** and **red**.

Say the rhyming words in the first box. Circle the letters that make the ending sound. Use the picture clue to write one more rhyming word.

bet pet met wet set let	**ending** en et ed	_____
fell tell bell sell	**ending** ess ell	_____
red fed led wed	**ending** et ed	_____
ten den pen men	**ending** en et	_____
best pest rest west test vest	**ending** est elt ent	_____

Name:_____ Date:_____

Review: Short Vowels

  Say the word in each space and listen for the vowel sound. Using the code, color the space that has the same vowel sound you hear in the word.

short **a** = (orange)   short **i** = (red)   short **u** = (green)

short **e** = (blue)   short **o** = (purple)   ☆ = (yellow)

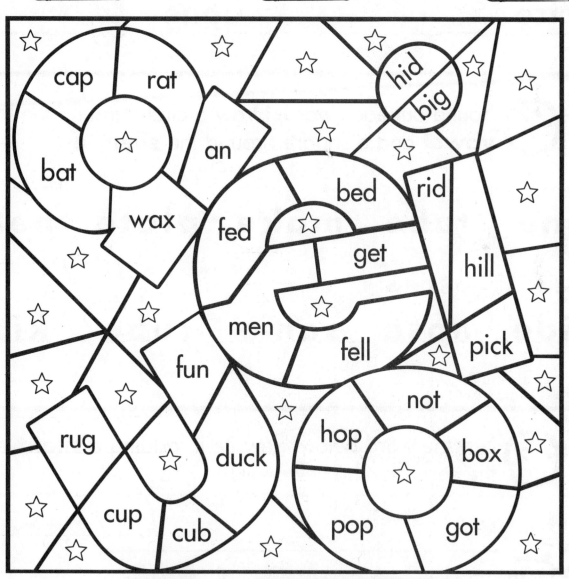

TAKE A BREAK! You did a great job!
Place your Book Mark here & RELAX!

Review: Short Vowels

27

Usually the vowel letter **e** is silent at the end of a word. The vowel letter that comes before it also has a long vowel sound.

Examples: cape, dime, rose, cube.

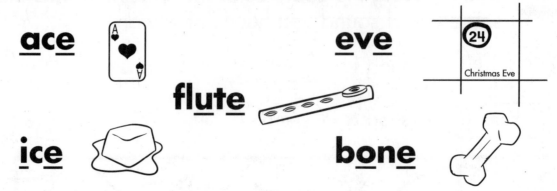

<u>a</u>c<u>e</u>

<u>e</u>v<u>e</u>

fl<u>u</u>t<u>e</u>

<u>i</u>c<u>e</u>

b<u>o</u>n<u>e</u>

  Sound out each word. Draw a circle around the **long vowel** and a square around the **silent e**.

line   tube   make   plate   here

hide   nose   same   cube   kite

  Say the word below. Rewrite it, adding a **silent e** at the end. Say the new word.

 _____ _____

man ------ ------

Say the name of each picture. Write the missing vowel and the silent **e** to complete each word.

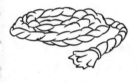

_____
r _ p _

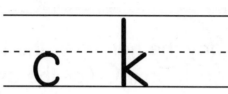
c _ k _

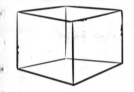
c _ b _

d _ c _
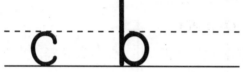

st _ v _

h _ v _
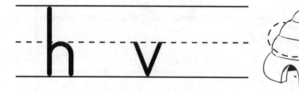

 Challenge: Write **pin, hop, cut,** and **can** on a piece of paper. Then, write the words again with a **silent e** at the end. Say your new words. Can you make more words like this?

The words **lake** and **train** have the long **a** sound.

lake   **train**

  Say the names of the two pictures in each box. Color the one with the long **a** sound.

Name:_____   Date:_____

Usually, **ai** has the long **a** sound.

nail

 **braid**

   Say the words in the box. Write a word from the box to complete each sentence. Circle **ai** in each word you write.

hail	rain	mail	pail	paint	laid

_____

The_____ **is full of**

_____ **.**

Will the clouds bring _____

or _____ **?**

I_____ **the**

_____ **on the table.**

Usually, **ay** has the long **a** sound.

h<u>ay</u>

 tr<u>ay</u>

 Say the words in the box. Write a word from the box to complete each sentence. Circle **ay** in each word you write.

clay	pay	day	play	gray	stay

_____

Every _____ I

_____ with friends.

I_____ inside when

the clouds are _____ .

Did you _____

for the _____ ?

The words **kite** and **light** have the long **i** sound.

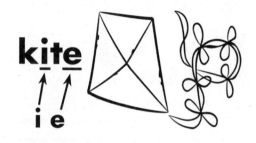

k<u>i</u>t<u>e</u>
↑ ↑
i e

l<u>igh</u>t
↑
igh

Tip:
Remember –
the long **i** vowel
sound is the same
as the letter's
name – **I**!

  Say the names of the two pictures in each box.
Color the one with the long **i** sound.

Usually, **ie** has the long **i** sound.

p<u>ie</u>

 **tie**

Usually, **igh** has the long **i** sound.

n<u>igh</u>t

 **r<u>igh</u>t**

 Draw an X on the word in each box that does <u>not</u> have the long **i** sound.

tie fight ~~fit~~	die did light
lie might fin	night pie pin
tight tin nice	bright tint sigh

The words **nose** and **coat** have the long **o** sound.

nose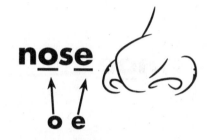

↑ ↑
o e

 **coat**

↑
oa

Tip:
Remember –
the long **o** vowel
sound is the same
as the letter's
name - **O**!

  Say the names of the two pictures in each box.
Color the one with the long **o** sound.

Usually, **oe** at the end of a word has the long **o** sound.

d<u>oe</u>   **h<u>oe</u>**

Usually, **oa** has the long **o** sound.

c<u>oa</u>st 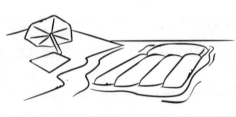 **fl<u>oa</u>t**

 Draw a line to match each word with the correct picture.

   **toe**   

boat

   **coal**

toast

soap

   **coat**   

When **o** is at the end of a word, it has the long **o** sound.

A green light means this car can **go, go, go!**

In some words, **ow** has the long **o** sound.

b<u>ow</u>

 **sn<u>ow</u>**

 Circle the long **o** word that best completes each sentence.

We will _____ to the store.

no	**go**	**so**

A big, black _____ is on the roof.

row	**low**	**crow**

Did the wind _____ the tree down?

mow	**blow**	**throw**

I like to sleep in my _____ bed.

own	**blown**	**grown**

The words **mule** and **fruit** have the long **u** sound.

Tip:
Remember – the long **u** vowel sound is the same as the vowel letter's name - **U**!

  Say the names of the two pictures in each box.
Color the one with the long **u** sound.

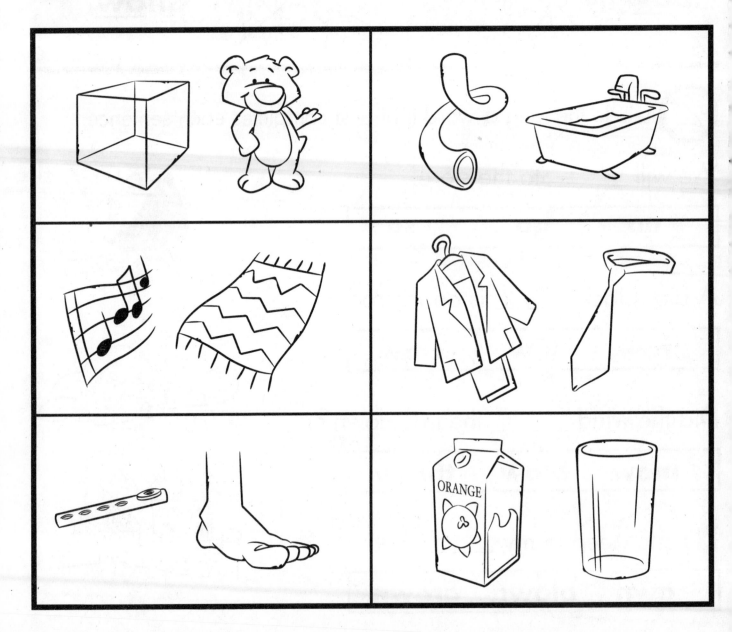

Usually, **ue** has the long **u** sound.

glue

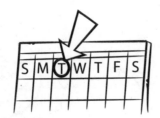 **Tuesday**

In some words, **ui** has the long **u** sound.

fruit

 **juice**

 Draw a line to match each word with the correct picture.

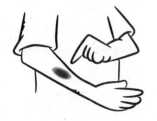

fruit

clue

glue

bruise

cruise

suit

The words **weed** and **meat** have the long **e** sound.

weed     **meat**

Tip:
Remember the long **e** sound is the same as the vowel letter's name - **E!**

  Say the names of the two pictures in each box.
Color the one with the long **e** sound.

Usually, **ea** has the long **e** sound.

leaf     **seal**

  Say the words in the box. Write one of the words on each line to complete the sentences.

meal	eat	tea	team	leap	cream

_____

We will_____our

_____ now.

_____

Everyone on the_____

can_____high.

_____

I put _____

in my_____.

When **e** is at the end of a word, it has the long **e** sound.

be   **he**   **sh<u>e</u>**   **m<u>e</u>**   **w<u>e</u>**

Usually, **ee** has the long **e** sound.

kn<u>ee</u>

   **m<u>ee</u>t**

 Circle the word that completes each sentence.

Spring will _____ here soon.

| **be** | **he** | **me** |

_____

Cars drive on the _____.

| **sleep** | **steep** | **street** |

How far can you _____?

| **see** | **seem** | **sheep** |

A _____ is on the flower.

| **feet** | **beef** | **bee** |

I _____ happy today.

| **fee** | **feel** | **free** |

Review: Long Vowels

Each girl is saying something. The missing words are on her house.

 Write the correct words to complete the sentences.

My cat is _____.

She has a pink _____.

nose
cute

I _____ **ice cream.**

It is good with _____.

cake
like

Dad will _____ **home soon.**

Then we will _____.

play
be

STOP! TAKE A BREAK! You did a great job! Place your Book Mark here & RELAX!

Some consonants can be put together to make a **blend**.

The **blend _dr_** has the sound you hear in the word <u>**drew**</u>.

The **blend _gr_** has the sound you hear in the word <u>**green**</u>.

The **blend _tr_** has the sound you hear in the word <u>**tree**</u>.

He <u>**drew**</u> a <u>**green**</u> <u>**tree**</u>.

 Say the words in the box. Use a word from the box to write the name of each picture.

bricks	dragon	crown	grass	train	prize

_____

- - - - - - - - - - - - - - - -

_____

_____

- - - - - - - - - - - - - - - -

_____

 Write two more words that have the consonant **r** blend.

_____

- - - - - - - - - - - - - - - -

_____

Recognizing and writing two-letter blends with **r**

Name:_____ Date:_____

The **blend _bl_** has the sound you hear in the word **<u>blue</u>**.
The **blend _pl_** has the sound you hear in the word **<u>planes</u>**.
The **blend _fl_** has the sound you hear in the word **<u>fly</u>**.

 Circle the **blends** at the beginning of each word.

clock     slide

glove     black

flag     plane

 Write four more words that have the consonant **l** blend.

_____   _____

- - - - - - - - - - - - -   - - - - - - - - - - - - -

_____   _____

- - - - - - - - - - - - -   - - - - - - - - - - - - -

_____   _____

Recognizing and writing two-letter consonant blends with l   **45**

Name:_____   Date:_____

The **blend _sp_** has the sound you hear in the word **<u>sp</u>ider**.
The **blend _st_** has the sound you hear in the word **<u>st</u>ory**.
The **blend _sc_** has the sound you hear in the word **<u>sc</u>ary**.

  Say the words in the box. Use a word from the box to write the name of each picture.

smile	snail	skate	sweater	stove	snow

_____

_____

_____

_____

_____

_____

 Write two more words that have the consonant **s** blend.

_____   _____

_____   _____

Recognizing and writing two-letter consonant blends with **s**

A word may begin or end with a **blend**.

skate   ma**sk**

  Say the words below. Circle the two-letter consonant **blend** at the end of each word.

ant	**must**	**felt**
band	**lamp**	**ink**
ask	**lift**	**last**
milk	**ring**	**pink**

 Use the words above to write the name of each picture.

_____   _____

Name:_____ Date:_____

Review: Blends

  Say each picture name. Write the correct beginning **blend** for each picture name.

_____

- - - - - - - - - - - - -

_____

_____

- - - - - - - - - - - - -

_____

_____

- - - - - - - - - - - - -

_____

_____

- - - - - - - - - - - - -

_____

_____

- - - - - - - - - - - - -

_____

_____

- - - - - - - - - - - - -

_____

_____

- - - - - - - - - - - - -

_____

_____

- - - - - - - - - - - - -

_____

_____

- - - - - - - - - - - - -

_____

One sound for **th** is heard in the words **the** and **mother**.

The other sound for **th** is heard in the words **thirty** and **teeth**.

mother

 **teeth**

 Say each word out loud. If it has the same **th** sound as **mother**, circle the . If it has the same **th** sound as **thirty**, circle the **30**.

thing		**30**
bath		**30**
there		**30**
thin		**30**
think		**30**
father		**30**

Name:_____   Date:_____

The sound for **sh** is heard at the beginning of **<u>sh</u>oe** and at the end of **fi<u>sh</u>**.

<u>sh</u>oe     **fi<u>sh</u>**

 Write **sh** to complete each word. Say the words. Draw a line to match the word to the correct picture.

 _____**irt**

di_____

fla_____

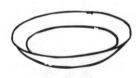 **bu_____**

_____**apes**

 **tra_____**

_____**op**

 _____**ark**

Recognizing the sound of consonant digraph **sh**

The sound for **ch** is heard at the beginning of <u>**ch**</u>**air** and at the end of **bran**<u>**ch**</u>.

<u>ch</u>air     **bran<u>ch</u>**

   Write **ch** to complete each word. Say the words. Draw a line from the word to the correct picture.

_____**eck**

ben_____

 _____**in**

tea_____**er**

 _____**ain**

in_____

 _____**est**

 _____**ur**_____

Name:_____ Date:_____

Review: Blends & Digraphs

  Say the word in each space. Color the picture using the code.

ch words = blue   **sh** words = green   **pl** words = pink

gr words = brown   **th** words = yellow

| path | math | play | plan | place | this |

think

there

cloth

they / then

shy / wish

that

those

with

truth

she

ash

mush

moth

the

green   grow   gray   group

great

inch   much

chin   chick

chat   such

grade

STOP! TAKE A BREAK! You did a great job!
Place your Book Mark here & RELAX!

Name:_____ Date:_____

A word that names a person, place, or thing is called a **noun**.

mother
person

home
place

purse
thing

 Write person, place, or thing under each picture to tell what kind of **noun** it names.

_____

_____

_____

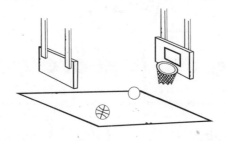

_____

_____

_____

_____

_____

_____

Name:_____ Date:_____

  Say each sentence out loud. Circle all the **noun** words you see.

The turtle lives in a pond.

 **The monkey has a tail.**

The giraffe eats leaves.

 **A zebra has stripes.**

The pilot sees a bird.

Ants make a tall hill.

Name:_____   Date:_____

A **verb** is a word that tells what a person or thing does.

 **run**    **spin**

 Challenge: Write some action words on small note cards. Pick a card and act out the action for a friend. Can your friend guess what you are doing? Then have your friend act a word out for you!

 Say each **verb** below. Draw a line to match the **verb** with the correct picture.

march

sing

dance

clap

 Circle the **verb** to complete each sentence.

The bell _____.

| soft | rings |

The cat _____.

| purrs | top |

Say each sentence out loud. Circle the **verb** in each sentence.

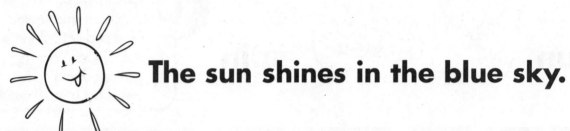

The sun shines in the blue sky.

Ships sail on the sea.

She sits in the sun.

Waves roll onto the shore.

They play a game.

He throws a ball.

Some sentences tell something. They are called **statements**.
A **statement** begins with a **capital letter** and ends with
a **period**.

capital letter

<u>T</u>he wind is strong.

period

  Say each sentence. Circle the **statement**.

Rain fell all day.

When will the rain stop?

  Say each sentence. Color in the ◯ by the **statement** that is written correctly.

◯ **today is a cold day.**
◯ **Today is a cold day.**

◯ **We like to play.**
◯ **do you like to play?**

◯ **The children made a snowman**
◯ **The children made a snowman.**

Some sentences ask something. They are called **questions**.
A **question** begins with a **capital letter** and ends with a
question mark.

capital letter   question mark

↘ <u>W</u>ho is it<u>?</u> ↙

  Say each sentence. Circle the questions.

What do you see?

The cat is in the tree.

Can it jump down?

 Rewrite each **question** so that it is correct.

what is your name

_____

- -

_____

how old are you

_____

- -

_____

where do you live

_____

- -

Review: Sentences & Questions

 Write your own **nouns** to complete the **sentences** and **questions** below.

1. For my birthday party, I would like to invite _____.

2. My favorite place to go is _____.

3. Do you know where my _____ is, Mom?

4. Do you have a _____ that I could borrow?

 Write your own **verbs** to complete the **sentences** and **questions** below.

5. On a nice day, I like to _____ with my friends at the playground.

6. Do you think we should _____ before we go to the mall?

7. Do you know how to _____?

8. If I owned a pig, I would _____ every day.

Name:_____   Date:_____

Review: Statements & Questions

 Write your own **statement** to describe the picture.

Challenge: Circle the **nouns** and underline the **verbs** in your **sentences** and **questions**!

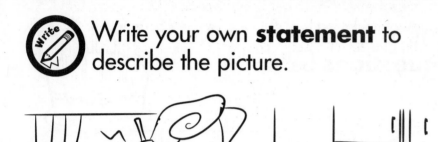

_____

_____

 Write your own **question** about the picture.

Tip:
Don't forget the correct capitalization and punctuation at the end of your **statements** & **questions**.

_____

_____

STOP! TAKE A BREAK! **You did a great job!**
Place your Book Mark here & RELAX!

Answer Key

Please take time to review the work your child or student has completed. Remember to praise both success and effort. If your child makes a mistake, let him or her know that mistakes are a part of learning. Explain why the incorrect response was not the best choice. Then, encourage your child to think it through and select a better choice.

page 3

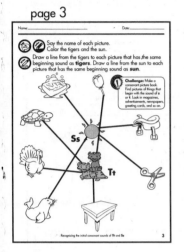

page 4

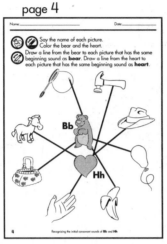

page 5

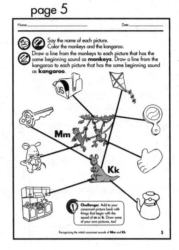

page 6

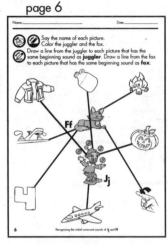

page 7

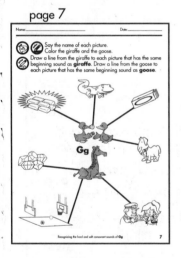

page 8

page 9

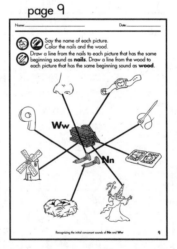

page 10

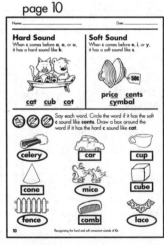

page 11

page 12

page 13

page 14

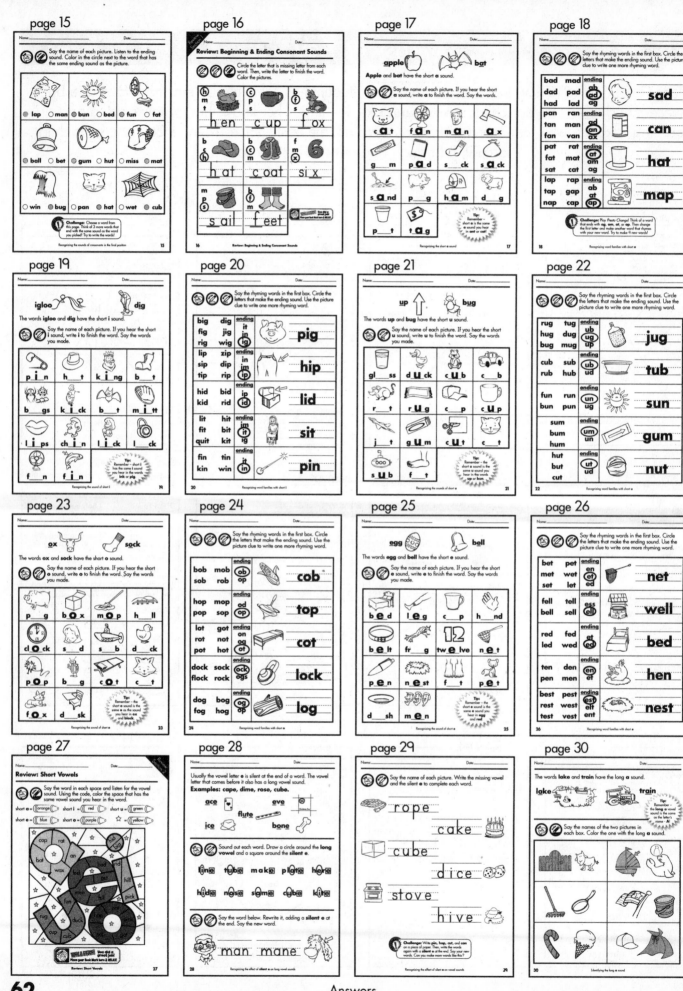

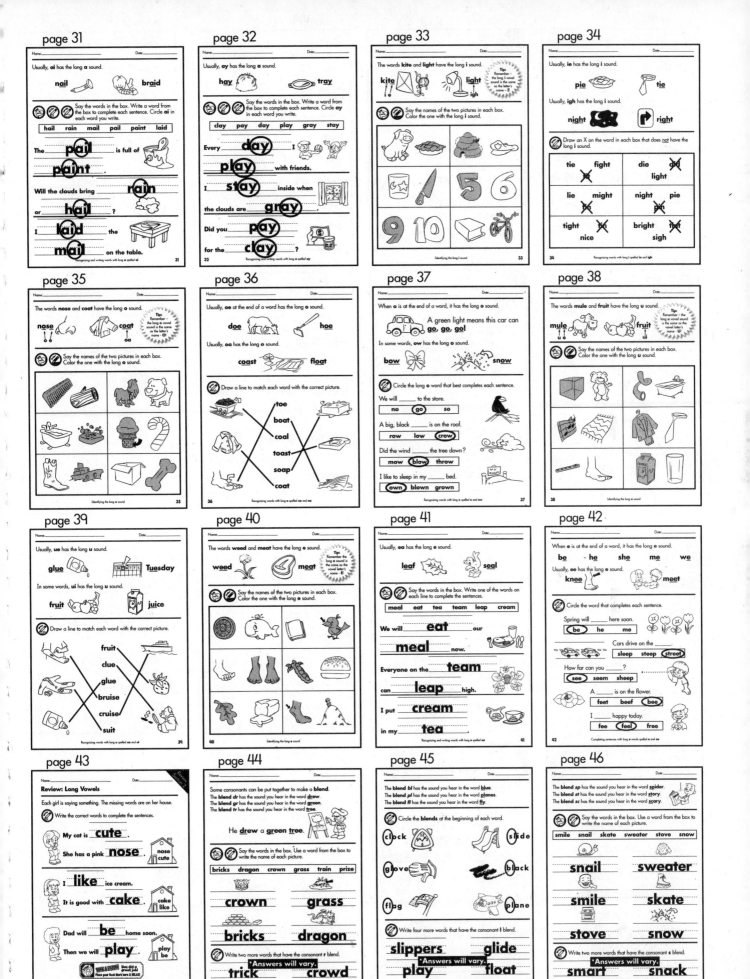

page 47

Name: _____ Date: _____

A word may begin or end with a **blend**.

skate   mask

Say the words below. Circle the two-letter consonant **blend** at the end of each word.

a(nt)   mu(st)   fe(lt)

ba(nd)   la(mp)   i(nk)

a(sk)   li(ft)   la(st)

mi(lk)   ri(ng)   pi(nk)

Use the words above to write the name of each picture.

lamp   **ant**

Recognizing two-letter blends in the final position   47

---

page 48

Name: _____ Date: _____

Review: Blends

Say each picture name. Write the correct beginning **blend** for each picture name.

sk   br   st

cl   cr   gl

fr   cr   sn

48   Review: Blends

---

page 49

Name: _____ Date: _____

One sound for **th** is heard in the words **the** and **mother**.

mother

The other sound for **th** is heard in the words **thirty** and **teeth**.

teeth

Say each word out loud. If it has the same **th** sound as **mother**, circle the ◯. If it has the same **th** sound as **thirty**, circle the **30**.

thing	◯	(30)
bath	(◯)	30
there	(◯)	30
thin	◯	(30)
think	◯	(30)
father	(◯)	30

Recognizing the two sounds of the consonant digraph th: voiced and unvoiced   49

---

page 50

Name: _____ Date: _____

The sound for **sh** is heard at the beginning of **shoe** and at the end of **fish**.

shoe   fish

Write **sh** to complete each word. Say the words. Draw a line to match the word to the correct picture.

sh irt
di **sh**
fla **sh**
bu **sh**
sh apes
tra **sh**
sh op
sh ark

50   Recognizing the sound of consonant digraph sh

---

page 51

Name: _____ Date: _____

The sound for **ch** is heard at the beginning of **chair** and at the end of **branch**.

chair   branch

Write **ch** to complete each word. Say the words. Draw a line from the word to the correct picture.

ch eck
ben **ch**
ch in
tea **ch** er
ch ain
in **ch**
ch est
ch ur **ch**

Recognizing the sound of the consonant digraph ch   51

---

page 52

Name: _____ Date: _____

Review: Blends & Digraphs

Say the word in each space. Color the picture using the code.

ch words = blue   sh words = green   pl words = pink
gr words = brown   th words = yellow

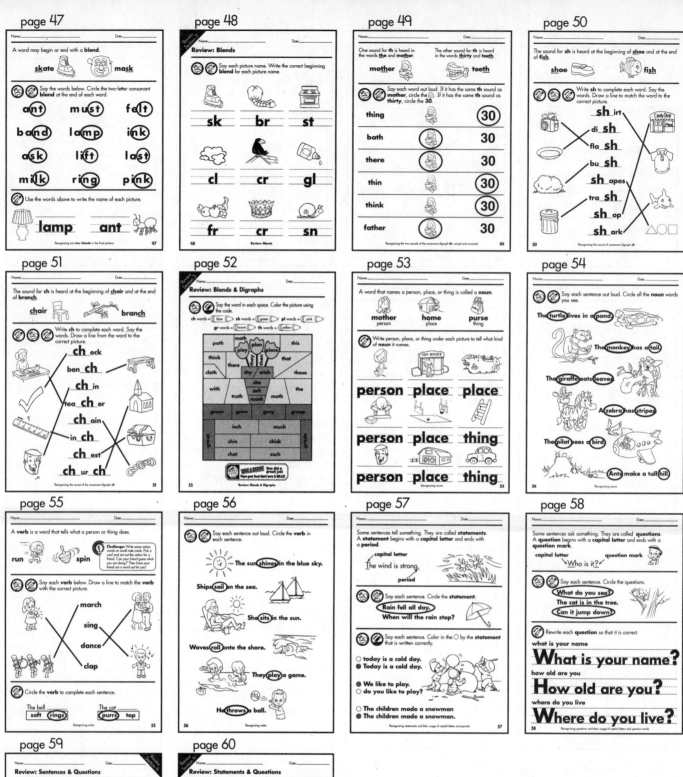

52   Review: Blends & Digraphs

---

page 53

Name: _____ Date: _____

A word that names a person, place, or thing is called a **noun**.

mother   home   purse
person   place   thing

Write person, place, or thing under each picture to tell what kind of **noun** it names.

person   **place**   **place**

person   **place**   **thing**

person   **place**   **thing**

Recognizing nouns   53

---

page 54

Name: _____ Date: _____

Say each sentence out loud. Circle all the noun words you see.

The (turtle) lives in a (pond).

The (monkey) has a (tail).

The (giraffe) eats (leaves).

A (zebra) has (stripes).

The (pilot) sees a (bird).

(Ants) make a tall (hill).

54   Recognizing nouns

---

page 55

Name: _____ Date: _____

A **verb** is a word that tells what a person or thing does.

run   spin

Challenge: Write some action words on small note cards. Pick a card and act out the action for a friend. Can your friend guess what you are doing? Then have your friend act a word out for you!

Say each **verb** below. Draw a line to match the **verb** with the correct picture.

march
sing
dance
clap

Circle the **verb** to complete each sentence.

The bell ____   soft (rings)

The cat ____   (purrs) top

Recognizing verbs   55

---

page 56

Name: _____ Date: _____

Say each sentence out loud. Circle the **verb** in each sentence.

The sun (shines) in the blue sky.

Ships (sail) on the sea.

She (sits) in the sun.

Waves (roll) onto the shore.

They (play) a game.

He (throws) a ball.

56   Recognizing verbs

---

page 57

Name: _____ Date: _____

Some sentences tell something. They are called **statements**. A **statement** begins with a **capital letter** and ends with a **period**.

capital letter
The wind is strong.
period

Say each sentence. Circle the **statement**.

(Rain fell all day.)
When will the rain stop?

Say each sentence. Color in the ◯ by the **statement** that is written correctly.

◯ today is a cold day.
● Today is a cold day.

● We like to play.
◯ do you like to play?

◯ The children made a snowman
● The children made a snowman.

Recognizing statements and their usage of capital letters and periods   57

---

page 58

Name: _____ Date: _____

Some sentences ask something. They are called **questions**. A **question** begins with a **capital letter** and ends with a **question mark**.

capital letter   question mark
Who is it?

Say each sentence. Circle the questions.

(What do you see?)
The cat is in the tree.
(Can it jump down?)

Rewrite each **question** so that it is correct.

what is your name
What is your name?

how old are you
How old are you?

where do you live
Where do you live?

58   Recognizing questions and their usage of capital letters and question marks

---

page 59

Name: _____ Date: _____

Review: Sentences & Questions

Write your own **nouns** to complete the **sentences** and **questions** below.

*Responses will vary.

1. For my birthday party, I would like to invite ____ **Mona**
2. My favorite place to go is ____ **the beach**
3. Do you know where my ____ **football** is, Mom?
4. Do you have a ____ **pen** that I could borrow?

Write your own **verbs** to complete the **sentences** and **questions** below.

5. On a nice day, I like to ____ **play** with my friends at the playground.
6. Do you think we ____ before we go to the mall? *Responses will vary.
7. Do you know how to ____ **water ski**?
8. If I owned a pig, I would ____ **laugh** every day.

Review: Sentences & Questions   59

---

page 60

Name: _____ Date: _____

Review: Statements & Questions

Write your own **statement** to describe the picture.

Challenge: Circle the **nouns** and underline the **verbs** in your **sentences** and **questions!**

*Responses will vary.
Mom is ordering pizza on her cell phone.

Write your own **question** about the picture.

Tip: Don't forget the correct capitalization and punctuation at the end of your **statements** & **questions.**

*Responses will vary.
What do you think dad is making?

60   Review: Statements & Questions

64

Answers

Letter Sound Search

1. Take the game board anywhere - look & listen for letter sounds!
2. When you see an object that begins with the same sound as a letter on the board, cover that space with a chip, a piece of paper, or a penny.
3. How quickly can you find all the letter sounds?

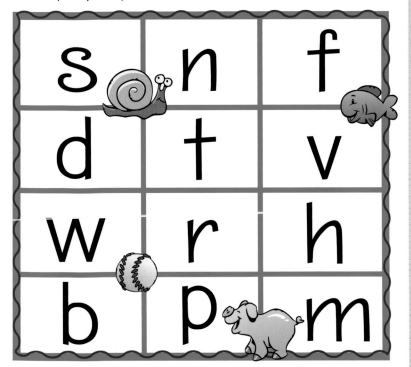

s	n	f
d	t	v
w	r	h
b	p	m

CUT HERE

Beginning Blend Search

1. Take the game anywhere & practice with beginning letter blends!
2. Read the words & when you see the object with the letter blend in its name, cover that space with a chip, a piece of paper, or a penny.
3. How quickly can you find all the beginning blends?

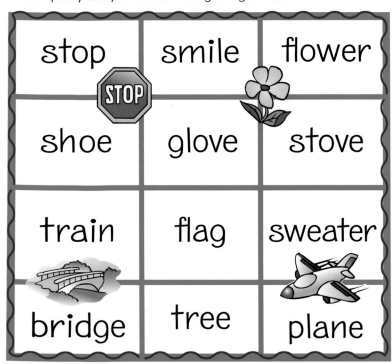

stop	smile	flower
shoe	glove	stove
train	flag	sweater
bridge	tree	plane

©2009 Learning Horizons, Inc.

YOUR NAME

SKILL CHECKLIST!

HOP HOP HOORAY!

Use this Skill Checklist to check off the skills as you practice them in the book.

- [ ] Beginning Consonant sounds
- [ ] Ending Consonant Sounds

- [ ] Short Vowel Families
- [ ] Long Vowel Families

- [ ] Beginning Blends
- [ ] Ending Blends

- [ ] Nouns & Verbs
- [ ] Writing Sentences

LONG VOWEL SEARCH

1. Take the game with you anywhere & find long vowels!
2. Read the words & when you see the object with the long vowel in its name, cover that space with a chip, a piece of paper, or a penny.
3. How quickly can you find all the long vowels?

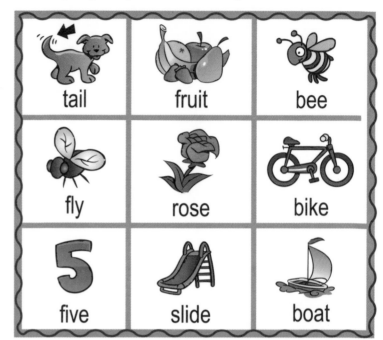

tail	fruit	bee
fly	rose	bike
five	slide	boat

CUT HERE

NOUN & VERB SEARCH

1. Take the game anywhere & look for nouns & verbs.
2. Read the words & when you see the object or someone showing the action, cover that space with a chip, a piece of paper, or a penny.
3. How quickly can you find all the nouns & verbs?

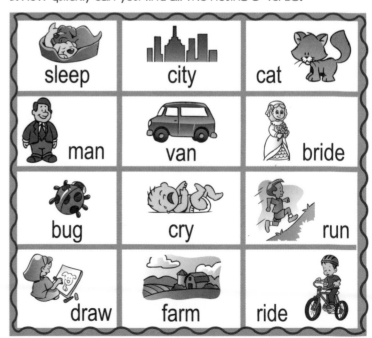

sleep	city	cat
man	van	bride
bug	cry	run
draw	farm	ride